W9-APU-098

Farewell to Steam

FAREWE

DAVID PLOWDEN

LL TO STEAM

BONANZA BOOKS · NEW YORK

FOR P. C. P.

ACKNOWLEDGMENTS

This book would not have been possible without the help given me by officials of steamboat and railroad operations in the United States and Canada, by members of the brotherhood of steam historians and enthusiasts, by engineers, firemen, hostlers, wheelmen, deckhands, chiefs, captains, train dispatchers and station agents. They are too numerous to list here, but to the following, for assistance above and beyond any expectable generosity, I would like to express particular gratitude—while claiming all errors as mine alone:

Mr. T. A. Armstrong, of the Canadian Pacific Railway's Port McNicoll, Ontario, end of the *Keewatin*'s and the *Assiniboia*'s operation; Capt. William Atkinson of the ferryboat *Orange*; Mr. Edw. J. Burns, Administrative Officer of the New York State Bridge Authority; Mr. Amos Cardova, agent of the Denver & Rio Grande Western Railroad, Durango, Colorado; the late Mr. K. R. Cobb, President of the Virginia Blue Ridge Railway; Miss E. Delarue, indomitable owner of the incomparable *Lone Star* of Davenport, Iowa, and Captain and Mrs. Johnson; Mr. William Dewan, of the Canadian National Railways' public relations department; Mr. George Eastland, of the public relations department of the Erie-Lackawanna Railroad; Mr. William Greene, roundhouse foreman, Canadian National Railways, Hamilton, Ontario; Mr. N. W. James, of the Central Railroad of New Jersey's public relations department; Miss Ann Kuss, of the New York Central System's public relations department, and Mr. William Navara, Superintendent of the NYCRR Marine Department; Mr. William Laidlaw, Chief Train Dispatcher Emeritus, Moosehead Subdivision of the Canadian Pacific Railway; Mr. C. Bradford Mitchell, Director of Information, the American Merchant Marine Institute, and noted marine historian and writer; Mr. Richard Mitchell, acknowledged authority on the marine reciprocating engine, and builder-owner of the lovely steam launch *River Queen*, of Hinsdale, New Hampshire; M. André Poloquin, of Canada Steamship Lines, Quebec; Mr. Bud Rolfe, Moosehead Subdivision engineer, Canadian Pacific Railway, and Mr. Douglas Blue, fireman; Mr. John Sangster, McAdam, New Brunswick, Roundhouse Foreman, the Canadian Pacific Railway; Capt. Neil Steevels, of the Erie-Lackawanna Railroad's Hoboken ferry line; Mr. Louis Weinstein, of the New York City Department of Marine & Aviation; Mrs. Juanita Williams, of the Memphis District office, U.S. Army Corps of Engineers; Mr. James T. Wilson, President of the Steamboat Historical Society of America; the late Capt. Donald T. Wright, editor of *The Waterways Journal;* and Mr. William S. Young, famed railroad historian, and publisher of *Steam Locomotive and Railroad Tradition* magazine.

And finally I thank my wife, and Janet Greene, senior editor of The Stephen Greene Press. D. P.

The steamboat on the Title-page is the *Richelieu*, operated on the St. Lawrence River by the Canada Steamship Lines. The steam locomotive is the Duluth, Missabe & Iron Range Railroad's No. 220, a type 2-8-8-4 Yellowstone, class M-3.

Copyright © MCMLXVI by David Plowden.
All rights reserved. No part of this book may be reproduced in any form without permission from the publisher, except by a reviewer who may quote brief passages.
Library of Congress catalog card number: 65–18369.
Printed in the United States of America.

This edition published by Bonanza Books,
a division of Crown Publishers, Inc.,
by arrangement with The Stephen Greene Press
b c d e f g h

CONTENTS

PROLOGUE

One of the most important events in the development of modern western civilization was the invention of the reciprocating steam engine, and indeed its impact on the course of North American history alone was as direct and powerful as its own mechanical action.

This creation is perhaps the simplest and most beautiful power mechanism that man has ever devised; to me all other machines pale by comparison. In elementary terms, it is an engine with cylinders (or one cylinder, in its most modest form) in each of which a piston travels straight back and forth—hence "reciprocating." Steam, admitted and exhausted alternately at both ends of the stroke, pushes the piston both forward and back, and makes each stroke a power stroke—a unique feature of the reciprocating engine. The force is transmitted directly from the piston to either a wheel or a crankshaft by a system of rods and cranks, creating a sublime precision of movement. The fact that there are no gears or transmission makes this the only engine with equal power both in forward and in reverse, and enables it to move anything so long as there is enough steam to push the piston.

Although this engine performed countless different jobs in industry and agriculture between the onset of the Industrial Revolution and the threshold of the Atomic Age, it was in transportation that reciprocating steam made its most outstanding contribution. Without it there would have been no steamboats to exploit the magnificent natural waterways of our continent, and there would have been no railroads to bind isolated communities of North America together into great national entities. Without it we would have had no Age of Steam.

Now this era is over, a scant century and a half after it began; and the symbol of the age—reciprocating steam—has been superseded in intracontinental water and land transport almost entirely by the internal combustion engine. Since World War II the survival of any machine depends increasingly on compact, push-button automation and by cost-accounting operation: it is one of the splendors of the reciprocating steam engine that it was, in comparison, both ravenous and extravagant. Generating steam in a boiler larger than the engine itself required mountains of fuel—and, in the case of locomotives, also vast stores of fresh water; then, all those beautiful moving parts absorbed most of the steam's power with each direct thrust; and finally, it demanded a host of men to perform the attendant rituals of service to maintain it and to run it.

Certainly these were drawbacks, but they were minor compared to the staggering economic handicap imposed on rail and domestic steamboat operations by the emergence of the private automobile as the foremost means of travel. Today in North America less than ten percent of the people journey by public transport at all, and then by airplane, bus, or, in ever decreasing numbers, by train; steamboats are not even cited in the comparative statistics. In addition, the business of carrying freight, while it does not reflect the passenger ratio, each year sees more trailer trucks moving goods on more interstate speedways.

It remains to be seen if the internal combustion engine can restore at least a part of steam's competitive position before the motorcar took over. Meanwhile our railroads and steamboat lines have rushed to embrace the Diesel in an effort to lure travelers and cargoes away from the superhighways and airlanes, and back to the continent's rails and waters.

Although some are earlier, most of the pictures that follow were taken around five years ago, when there remained enough old-time reciprocating steam to let me choose examples that could evoke the feeling of an all but vanished way of life. I was intent on offering a memoir of impressions, rather than trying to compile an illustrated encyclopedia of all reciprocating machinery extant, complete with details for the expert. And, while I was always aware that the individuals before my camera were living on borrowed time, I did not go deliberately to home ports or railroad yards with the purpose of recording a last season, a last run; yet this is exactly what a saddening number of my self-imposed assignments have, in retrospect, turned out to be.

This is a collection of photographs of steamboats—so often neglected in this context—and steam locomotives while they were still doing the work that created an era. It began as a personal salute, and has ended as a farewell to the Age of Steam.

DAVID PLOWDEN

New York City
February 1966

STEAMBOATS

It seems logical to begin with boats, for several reasons: Robert Fulton's *North River Steamboat* (popularly known as the *Clermont*) was launched in 1807, thus predating our first operating steam railroad by twenty-odd years; and even now examples from the heyday of the reciprocating engine—thin though their ranks may be—can be found working on some waterways.

Diversification has certainly played a part in this survival. The new form of transport was put to many uses after it was first introduced as the means to travel straight upstream against a river's current. As it spread to all our continent's navigable waters and was adapted to an increasing variety of services, the steamboat *per se* was refined into a number of categories. There was overnight and day excursion steamers, and packets carrying passengers, mail and goods on regularly scheduled runs; there were ferries taking people to and from work; vessels for carrying particular kinds of freight; boats designed for transferring cargo, or hauling or shoving barges, or for clearing channels.

Powered by reciprocating steam and first driven always by paddlewheels and later almost entirely by propellers, they plied our coasts, crisscrossed our lakes and harbors, and caused whole towns to spring up along our rivers wherever they were accustomed to nose in to the banks to load and unload.

The differentiating feature of all these steamboats can be described most simply as architectural, because their specific function dictated their configuration. For instance, the day excursion steamer had many open decks so passengers could take the air and admire the view; the luxurious overnight steamer was in effect a floating hotel, having tiers of state-rooms surrounding magnificent public parlors; and, because its job was to be a highly maneuverable source of power, the tug was essentially just an engine in a hull with a pilothouse.

The overall design was modified by other factors, as well. One was geography—the climate, or the type of waters traveled. The high-sided winter ferry crossing the St. Lawrence River had sharp prows to cut the ice and was armor-clad to withstand the pressure of the flows. The ferry on shallow Western rivers like the Mississippi, the Red, and the Ohio was a catamaran with next to no draft, and a paddlewheel housed in the center of the boat between the twin hulls. Peculiar to many North American boats on sheltered waters was the sponson, a projection of the bottom deck and superstructure overhanging the sides of the hull; it increased the carrying space without widening the hull and cutting down the speed of the boat.

The other modifier was the means of propulsion, so noticeable in paddlewheel boats.

Almost dominating the profile of our sidewheelers were the mammoth paddleboxes, often thirty or more feet in diameter, which encased the wheels above decks. They were installed mainly to confine the unbelievable splashing as the buckets thrashed the water, partly to muffle the noise, and incidentally to prevent passengers from falling into the wheels. During the Victorian period these semicircular expanses were decorated in the radiantly uninhibited taste of the times, but the grand old *Lansdowne* has unadorned paddleboxes. Nor does she have the walking beam—that fascinating diamond-shaped arm which rocked back and forth above the topmost deck of our classic sidewheelers. The last walking-beam engine ceased working in North America a decade ago.

The sternwheeler had no comparable paddlebox. Described as "able to run in a light dew on the grass," she was designed for shallow waters where formal landing piers seldom existed. Her single wheel at the stern—nearly as wide as the hull itself—was completely open to view, offering an inescapable demonstration of sheer power. Nowhere was the means of a boat's propulsion so wonderfully obvious as it was in the locomotive-like turning of this mighty wheel.

In the center-paddlewheeler, however, the relatively smaller wheel was moved up amidships between the twin hulls of the catamaran; and there it churned in a paddlebox concealed by the superstructure.

Perhaps the best-known vessels modified to a high degree by the combined factors of propulsion, geography and function were those passenger boats designated architecturally as "Steamboat Gothic." Especially notable on the Mississippi River complex, they were paddlewheelers; catering to newly wealthy travelers during the heyday of the gothic revival in the 1870's and '80's, their superstructures paraphrased the eclectic design and unabashed opulence of contemporary buildings ashore. Some had ballrooms. Some, too, had chapels, complete with organs, where Sunday services were led by the captain. Many of the day boats had dining saloons whose appointments matched the deliberate gorgeousness of Society's favorite restaurants on land.

No authentic Steamboat Gothic remains afloat today, since the only acknowledged classic Mississippi riverboat now operating is a modest vessel with no pretentions to grandeur as she pushes barges on short hauls up- and downstream. Nevertheless even in some of the region's passenger boats built from early in World War I to the mid-1920's, one can see features that indicate a family resemblance handed down from the luxury steamers of nearly a century ago—a paddlewheel, a boxy superstructure, the hint of a Texas deck, a slender feathered stack.

Modification according to service and locale also makes it impossible to set any one date as marking the end of paddlewheels and the beginning of propellers, and the boats in this book reflect the difficulty. The oldest, built in 1875, is screw-driven; the next-to-youngest, built in 1940, is a stern-wheeler. Not counting snagboats or dredgers, of the three sidewheelers still working on the continent as I write, I have chosen two; of the half-dozen sternwheelers, I show three; and I have pictured all four center-paddlewheelers. The rest of the boats on these pages are driven by propellers.

Since this book is not intended to trace the evolution of the reciprocating marine engine from its inception to its most sophisticated form, I shall say only that a definite change in steamboat architecture was produced by the introduction of a practical propeller combined with the development of the high-pressure boiler and the efficient compound engine utilizing a condenser. These innovations meant that the superstructure no longer needed to accommodate paddle-wheels or the mechanical system that moved them. Because the screw had to operate farther below the waterline, the propeller shaft and the more compact engine that powered it were placed deep in the hull. The center of gravity was visibly, as well as actually, much lower; and of course extra cargo space was created below decks. The counterstern, that lovely outward swell of the stern above the waterline, was a classic feature of large early propeller-driven vessels. In the inevitable march of technology the reciprocating engine has been replaced by the steam turbine and the Diesel in marine use. Virtually all our turbines have been installed in large ocean-going ships, while the internal combustion engine has taken over in the smaller boats like the ones represented in these pages.

The continent's last steamboat of any kind to be powered by reciprocating steam was built in 1957. Out of the thousands of such vessels that used to ply hundreds of lakes, only on the Great Lakes can they be found today; these, with the exception of a mere handful, are bulk-cargo carriers. Moreover, where they came and went on every navigable river, now they exist on only half a dozen. They are virtually extinct along our coasts too, and Long Island Sound—once the greatest steamboat showcase in North

America—has only one, a ferry steamer carrying automobiles. No ferries of any sort exist in San Francisco Bay, where they formerly clogged the harbor; two excursion steamers operate out of New York Harbor, but there were forty-five a quarter-century ago. Canada no longer has overnight luxury steamers running on the Great Lakes, and the ones on the St. Lawrence River have been withdrawn. The United States has two overnight passenger boats left, and only one sizable fleet of steam tugs.

The survivors are a strange assortment which, like the aged veterans of old wars, are often obscure individuals now regarded as heroic because of their longevity rather than for their deeds in battle. A number of steamboats continue to exist because in some capacity, however small, their operation is deemed worthwhile enough to keep them going even though it is not successful enough to encourage their owners to invest in new equipment. Others, especially ferries, are obliged to linger on for the duration of the complicated proceedings that follow petitions to abandon any public service; kept running long after their ownership has ceased to earn back the cost of their upkeep, they endure in a state of limbo—unpainted, unpatronized, unwanted. Still others have been granted a little more time by being picked up second-hand from a defunct service and transferred to distant waters to do jobs very different from the ones they were built for.

From this assortment I have chosen the boats that seem to me to reflect their functions most honestly, and I have grouped them according to their use when I found them and took their pictures. Not included are either individuals which, though powered by their original reciprocating engines, have been so remodeled and streamlined as to have lost their architectural identity and integrity, or individuals which have suffered the reverse process and have been subjected to artificial "periodization."

Also not included are some fine post-World War II reciprocating steamboats whose lines are so thoroughly modern that they look like Diesel-driven vessels; they belong to the present, not to the old romantic days of steam.

PASSENGER STEAMERS

The Golden Age of Steamboating, the late nineteenth into the early twentieth century, was epitomized by the splendid passenger steamers that served as packets, overnight boats or day boats on all the continent's navigable waters. Whether miniature liners crossing the Great Lakes or excursion steamers carrying patrons for just a few hours, these vessels combined luxury and the excitement of travel in a manner that has never been equaled by any other form of transport.

But no longer. Passenger steamboats, more than any other marine category, have seen their use decline almost to the

vanishing point. The storied Fall River Line of overnight boats succumbed before World War II; the last true packet run in the United States—perhaps the last in North America —finally gave up in 1962; and the day boats have fared little better.

This section contains my choice from the handful of surviving passenger boats, subdivided as the overnight steamer, the day excursion boat and the ferry steamer. The most familiar carrier of all, the shuttling passenger ferry, is treated separately later on.

OVERNIGHT LUXURY STEAMER

The overnight luxury steamers that lingered for a while after World War II were usually erstwhile packets whose beautiful sleeping accommodations allowed them to be used as cruise boats during the tourist season in summer. Some followed their old routes even when they no longer offered their former daily scheduled service.

By the time I set out to photograph the overnight reciprocating-steam boat in the United States and Canada, there were only seven survivors left to choose from: three on the Great Lakes, three on the St. Lawrence River, and one on the Mississippi System.

The *South American*, United States-owned, was still cruising between Buffalo and Duluth, but because of their greater age I chose the superlative *Keewatin* and *Assiniboia*

to represent the Great Lakes, and photographed the *Richelieu, Tadoussac* and *St. Lawrence* running from Montreal to the Saguenay, and the sternwheeler *Delta Queen* as she cruised the Mississippi.

Scarcely a year later, however, Canada passed a law that required replacement of wooden accommodations on all passenger vessels within the Dominion's waters. And then, before any appeals could be decided, there came the *Yarmouth Castle*'s disastrous fire at sea in November 1965.

So at this writing the *Keewatin*, the *Assiniboia*, and the fine St. Lawrence River trio have already been retired for good from passenger service. To offset such losses, there is small comfort in the reports that a second overnight steamboat may be added on the Mississippi.

4

PORT MC NICOLL DOCK

5

ASSINIBOIA

KEEWATIN

KEEWATIN

KEEWATIN

6

KEEWATIN

Sisters, and both built Clydeside in 1907 for the Canadian Pacific Railway, the *Keewatin* and *Assiniboia* are our most perfect examples of the propeller-driven luxury vessel from steamboating's golden age. These miniature liners—untainted by "modernization" and magnificently maintained through their very last day of passenger service—belong to the era of Grand Hotels and four-stacked "greyhounds of the sea." They are also the only examples that remained of the once-familiar Great Lakes passenger steamer with funnel aft.

The *Keewatin* was one of the continent's last few coal-burning overnight steamers, and her extraordinarily high stack is the dominant feature of her silhouette. She is down at the stern because her bunkers are full of coal as she starts across Lake Huron for Fort William on Lake Superior, two nights and a day away. *Assiniboia*'s shorter stack indicates that she was recently converted to oil—a fact that may save her from being scrapped.

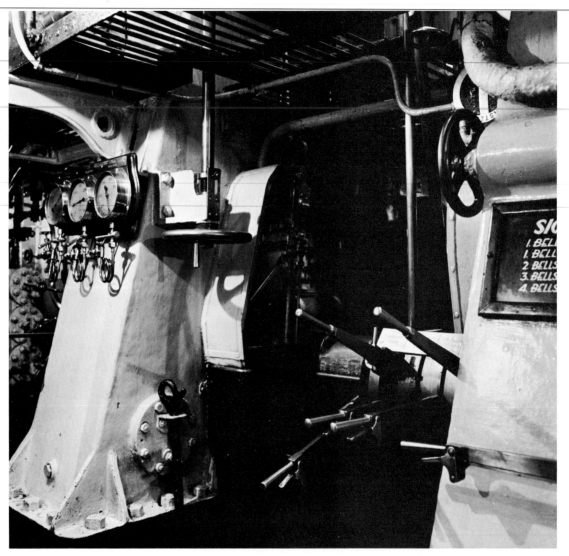

KEEWATIN: ENGINEROOM

ASSINIBOIA: TO THE WRITING ROOM

KEEWATIN: DINING SALOON

ASSINIBOIA: FLOWER WELL

11

KEEWATIN: BOUND FOR FORT WILLIAM

RICHELIEU

Richelieu . . . Tadoussac . . . St. Lawrence—their names evoke French Canada's heritage: where could they be but on the Dominion's greatest river? Yet their claim on our imaginations is more than geographic, for they were the only fleet of river steamers left in North America, and the continent's last boats which could possibly be called packets.

The *Richelieu* had the most dramatic career of the three. Designed by famed naval architect Frank E. Kirby, she was built in Delaware in 1913 in hopes of being part of a direct rail-steamer service between New York and Montreal. The plan fell through; she languished; acquired by the U.S. Navy as a troop transport during World War I and severely damaged in the English Channel, she limped home across the Atlantic on her own steam. Whereupon she was bought by Canada Steamship Lines, who changed her name from *Narragansett* to *Richelieu*, restored her luxurious prewar accommodations, and soon after the war placed her on the St. Lawrence. There her younger running-mates joined her a decade later.

The *Tadoussac* and *St. Lawrence* were built in 1929, and remained in the same service and on the same routes for which they were originally designed.

Even before Canada's 1965 law against wooden superstructures, economic pressures were forcing the decision to withdraw these stunning four-deckers from round-trip service from Montreal to deep in the mouth of the Saguenay River. Now only a miracle can save them from the scrapheap.

13

ST. LAWRENCE RIVER AT QUEBEC

RICHELIEU

RICHELIEU

RICHELIEU: WHEELHOUSE

TADOUSSAC: OFF ILE AUX COUDRES

AT MURRAY BAY

LEAVING ST-SIMÉON

25

ON THE MISSISSIPPI

26

The *Delta Queen*, the only overnight passenger steamer still working on any North American river, is a paradox: aside from her sternwheel, her name and her cruises on the Mississippi System, she is completely unlike the riverboats immortalized by Mark Twain.

Even so, I hope she will be joined by a new paddlewheeler to be driven, the rumors say, by the engines salvaged from the abandoned *Delta King*, her twin.

BELOW ROCK ISLAND

28

DELTA QUEEN

29

DAY EXCURSION STEAMER

Most of our surviving passenger steamboats fall into the excursion category, operating regularly for sightseers, or sometimes on chartered outings, or sometimes just poking around to pick up fares at a different port each day. In most cases even the crew sleeps ashore after the vessels tie up for the night.

The emphasis of the day steamer's design was on seeing-space rather than sleeping-space, but many had day staterooms as well as parlors and lavishly decorated dining saloons. This was the era when businessmen commuted on the "Palatial Steel Steamers" of the old Hudson River Day Line, or captains whistled once for every ten passengers to let the chef at the Grand Hotel know how many trippers were disembarking for lunch.

Today's boats lead a rackety sort of life, yet as long as enough sights are left unspoiled, and enough people want to leave jammed highways to see them, the day excursion boat, unlike the overnight steamer, might possibly continue its hand-to-mouth existence.

Of the boats that are left I have chosen three that I think give the most valid idea of the class. Many of the other survivors have been so extensively modernized—with airflow lines, chopped-up interiors, snack bars—or made so artificial in an attempt to provide an overlay of "period" style, that they are not representative of either today or yesterday.

BELLE OF LOUISVILLE: CYLINDER HEAD

ON THE OHIO

DOWNSTREAM FROM LOUISVILLE

The *Belle of Louisville* is a tramp. Built in Pittsburgh in 1914, she started life as a ferry, then operated as a towboat and as a packet. In 1962 she was stripped and sold at auction to Jefferson County, Kentucky. Dolled up and renamed, she now junkets sedately on the Ohio around Louisville.

All the illustrious vessels that overshadowed her are gone, so with her pilothouse amidships and vestige of a Texas deck, the *Belle* has emerged from obscurity to become the only passenger boat that bears even the slightest resemblance to the great Mississippi River steamers of old.

33

The Mississippi and the Hudson rivers are each famed for having developed a distinctive style of passenger steamboat. Today all the true Mississippi steamers have vanished, but on the Hudson there remains a lone and superb example: the *Alexander Hamilton*. Unquestionably the finest excursion steamer in North America—indeed, one of the few classic steamboats of any type that remain—she is the rightful heir to the Hudson River tradition.

She was built in 1924, yet her lines, with sidewheels concealed, are virtually identical with the prototype designed right after the turn of the century. Her original owner was the renowned Hudson River Day Line, whose home-flag emblem still adorns her twin stacks.

Each summer the *Alexander Hamilton* churns 144 miles a day on her round trips from New York City to Poughkeepsie; and, though her owners have given her extensive repairs, each September's final run raises the question of whether she will have another season. Thus it is heartening to hear faint rumors that the old HRDL's screw-driven *Peter Stuyvesant* may be returned to service in 1967 as her running-mate.

HUDSON RIVER DAY LINE

HEADING BACK TO NEW YORK

37

AT BEAR MOUNTAIN LANDING

38

DOWN THE BAY FOR JERSEY

UPRIVER CHARTER

FERRY STEAMER

LONG ISLAND SOUND

With ample deck space, and often with staterooms, the ferry steamer outwardly resembles a small passenger boat, but its prime function is to shuttle travelers and their automobiles across wide stretches of water.

The *Catskill*, formerly a freight boat on the Hudson, makes four daily round trips between Bridgeport, Connecticut, and Port Jefferson, Long Island, and has the distinction of being the only steamer still working regularly on Long Island Sound.

The best example of ferry steamer remaining on the East Coast is the *Nobska*, which has been running out of Woods Hole, Massachusetts, for Martha's Vineyard and Nantucket islands for thirty years. Although her own future is uncertain, it is likely that steam will remain for a while on this service: her running-mate is *Nantucket* (1957), the last boat in North America to be built with reciprocating engines.

NOBSKA: BOUND FOR NANTUCKET

SPARTAN

GREAT

DIAMOND ALKALI

LAKES

CARGO BOAT

Today one can still see coal smoke on the horizons of the Great Lakes, for it is in this region that reciprocating steam is waging its most valiant rear-guard action. And, fittingly, this defense is being fought by vessels indigenous to the area: the "Lakers"—the old straight-decked bulk-cargo carriers—and the great railroad-car ferries.

Since the turn of the century to the opening of the St. Lawrence Seaway the Lakers reigned—forming a conveyor belt each shipping season to bring grain and iron ore down from the top of Superior, carrying back steel and coal from Chicago, Detroit or the Lake Erie ports, and making the "Soo" locks between Lakes Huron and Superior the busiest in the world. Typical of these doughty bulk carriers are the *William J. Filbert*, the *Algosoo* and the *Diamond Alkali*.

This trio was built between 1901 and 1917 and, like other old steamboats still working in this region, owe their longevity partly to fresh-water operation. Their function is being challenged with increasing success, however, by the new breed of giant Diesel carrier fostered by the Seaway.

The picture opposite (and in the distance on page 44) shows the *Spartan*, a modern railroad-car ferry with passenger accommodations, and the youngest boat in this book. Built in 1952, she and a sister are probably the last coal-burning passenger boats launched in North America. She is almost streamlined compared with her famed old counterparts that follow.

WILLIAM J. FILBERT: NEAR STRAITS OF MACKINAC

LUDINGTON, MICHIGAN

ALGOSOO: COUNTERSTERN

RAILROAD-CAR FERRY

Among the most distinctive of our steamboats is the railroad-car ferry that still remains in force on Lake Michigan. It is noted for two things: its cavernous hull, capable of swallowing up entire trains, and—because it must operate through the severe Great Lakes winters—its prowess as an ice-breaker.

At this writing the Ann Arbor, the Chesapeake & Ohio, and the Grand Trunk Western railways maintain eight ferry routes on Lake Michigan, which juts several hundred miles into the industrial Midwest and severs otherwise continuous east-west rail lines. This ferry service therefore is indispensable to the region's transportation network, and doubtless will outlive the ferry on short crossings by many years—especially since an increasing percentage of its revenue derives from providing sleeping and dining facilities for motorists with their automobiles, who find the brief voyage a pleasant respite from problems of traffic on the speedways. There are boats on similar service operating between Seattle and Alaska.

In contrast to the sleek new *Spartan* (page 47), which typifies the latest trend in passenger accommodation, I have pictured two of the four boats belonging to the Ann Arbor Railroad, whose four crossings, radiating from Frankfort far up on Michigan's lower peninsula, have the greatest combined mileage of the three companies. They are *Ann Arbor No. 5*, built in 1910, and her running-mate, *Ann Arbor No. 7*, seventeen years younger. When photographed in 1963 both were carrying motorists in addition to freight cars. *No. 5* was designed by Frank E. Kirby, who also designed the famed *Richelieu*, shown earlier, and the heroic *Chief Wawatam*, coming in a minute. At that time the oldest railroad-car ferry on the open waters of the Lakes and a renowned ice-breaker, *No. 5* was even then used as a spare boat; at this writing she is laid up at Frankfort while her owners decide whether an increase in traffic will warrant her going to work again.

If she does, I hope that her age will preclude the expense of changing her. *No. 7* as pictured here is a perfect example of the old standard type, but recently she was considered young enough to be worth the cost of Diesel-izing and such extensive remodeling that she is unrecognizable.

ANN ARBOR NO. 7

SOO LINE DOCKS, MANITOWOC, WISCONSIN

ANN ARBOR NO. 5

OUT ACROSS LAKE MICHIGAN

ANN ARBOR NO. 5: COMING IN TO MANITOWOC

Built beside Ann *Arbor No. 5* in Toledo, since 1911 the bow-loading *Chief Wawatam* has plied the Straits of Mackinac where Lakes Michigan and Huron join to create the most wicked of all winter ferry crossings. Here this grand old lady of the Lakes has had to cope with piles of windrowed ice up to forty feet deep. But even she has not always made it: once she was imprisoned for one hundred days; and she always carries extra provisions in winter—although not so many now as in the years when she ferried the elite Lake Superior Limited and its passengers. Today she carries only freight cars.

In 1965 she underwent extensive repairs, and her new lease on life means that the floes piling across the Straits will not go unchallenged by this noble icebreaker.

CHIEF WAWATAM

LOADING AT MACKINAW CITY

57

RIVER
RAILROAD-CAR FERRY

The railroad-car carrier on the Detroit and St. Clair rivers is always treated separately, for not only is it quite different structurally from the Great Lakes ferry, but also in its ranks are two truly historic vessels—the *Lansdowne* and the *Huron*. The *Huron* was built in 1875, but has a propeller; the *Lansdowne* is a four-stacked sidewheeler built in 1884, with engines dating to 1872; both are iron-hulled; and between them they carry freight cars of automobile frames from Detroit to Windsor, Ontario, all year.

But here's what these bald facts amount to as I write:

The *Lansdowne* is the oldest working paddleboat in North America, and one of the oldest in the world. Her engines—one to each wheel, allowing independent operation and therefore maximum maneuverability—are the oldest pieces of reciprocating steam machinery engaged in transportation on the continent.

The *Huron* is by far the oldest steamboat in the Lakes region and, so far as is known, could be the oldest operating reciprocating-steam vessel in North America; certainly she is one of the oldest in the world. What is possibly the oldest steam tug in North America, the screw-driven *Seguin*, still works as a spare boat at Belfast, Maine; but she has the same date as the *Lansdowne*—1884.

Working in fresh water and having durable hulls that outlast modern steel have contributed to the *Lansdowne*'s and *Huron*'s longevity. Another factor is their long seasonal vacations: *Lansdowne* is the regular boat only in winter, when her sidewheels churn the slips free of ice, and the *Huron* works only in summer. In addition, the Canadian National Railways, their owner, maintains them magnificently. Thus while other steam machines fall victim to Detroit's automobile industry, these two wonderful boats perform the self-preserving function of carrying motorcar frames from place to place.

BACKING FROM THE SLIP

LANSDOWNE: PORTSIDE PADDLEBOX

EARLY APRIL

61

SEPTEMBER CROSSING TO DETROIT

ON OF SARNIA

COMING IN EMPTY AT WINDSOR

COMING IN EMPTY AT WINDSOR

The *Manitowoc* is a good example of the modern steam railroad-car ferry on the Detroit and St. Clair rivers. She is one of three operated by the Norfolk & Western Railroad between Detroit and Windsor.

63

WORKBOATS

The yeomen of the marine world are workboats like the tug, lighter, towboat, dredger and snagboat, which spend their lives doing essential chores without fanfare.

Most familiar is the harbor tug, whose design always stresses maneuverability and power because it must push, shove and pull barges or ocean liners with equal ease. The towboat has no distinctive shape: many different kinds of boats have nosed a tow upstream on our big Western rivers. And it doesn't haul a tow, it shoves it: but it's still called a towboat.

The lighter seems rather like a long-nosed tug with a crane. The dredger and the snagboat look only like themselves.

TUG

Typical of the small harbor tugboat of the past are the dozen-odd vessels used by the New York Central System to move its cargo barges and car floats around New York Harbor. The last sizable fleet of the steam tugs in North America, these stanch little performers will no doubt be retired when the NYCRR-Pennsylvania merger allows the Pennsy's new Diesel tugs to take over.

The oldest NYCRR tug shown was built in 1901, the youngest in 1924. Since they were photographed, something prompted the company to paint them a sickly green; it mars their dignity—superficially.

NEW YORK HARBOR

OFF THE NORTH RIVER PIERS

NYCRR MARINE SHOP

NYCRR NO. 18

NYCRR NO. 10

Last of the old Delaware, Lackawanna & Western's steam tugs, the *Bronx* is here nearly fifty years old, yet worked a daily round trip from Hoboken to the line's Bronx warehouse. Her stubby stack lets her scoot beneath the Harlem River's many low bridges.

LIGHTER

The steam lighter's shape is interesting to photograph, but she has a purpose beyond being starkly decorative: her job is to aid ships not able to find berths by loading or lightening them of their cargo, and puffing away with it to various parts of the harbor.

The mundane variety of lighter, merely an unpowered barge with a crane, is plentiful around our ports; any kind of self-propelled one is a rarer species; but rarest of all is the steam-driven lighter—of which the three in New York Harbor are possibly the only ones left on the entire continent.

One of these is *Victor*, belonging to the Petterson Lighterage & Towing Corporation. If you're lucky, you may see her slipping around The Battery through the mists of early morning.

AT THE BATTERY

75

VICTOR

TOWBOAT

There are possibly three sternwheel steam towboats left in North America, and one of them is the *Lone Star*. Wooden-hulled, coal-fired, twin-stacked—she is acknowledged to be the only classic Mississippi boat left to us today. Mark Twain would have loved her.

Her hull, built in 1890, establishes her official age; her superstructure, though of a later date, is perfectly in keeping with her era. She noses barges of sand or gravel a few miles up- and downstream from Davenport, Iowa, or syphons sand from the bottom of her river. The firemen double as deckhands, the captain's wife cooks in her little galley between the engines, and the engineer's dog goes along for the ride. Everyone takes a personal interest in her well-being, with the result that her ancient parts are kept running as if by love alone.

Fifty years ago *Lone Star* would have been commonplace on the big river, but now she alone carries on the tradition of true Mississippi steamboating.

ON THE ILLINOIS SIDE BELOW DAVENPORT

79

LONE STAR

STE. GENEVIEVE: NEAR CAIRO

DREDGER
AND SNAGBOAT

To be puristical about it, dredgers are not regarded as boats, since—even when self-propelled—they are not transports. For interest, though, I include two examples from a number owned by the U.S. Army Corps of Engineers, which maintains almost all of America's inland waterways and keeps the channels of navigable rivers clear. Both on the Mississippi, they are the sternwheeled *Ste. Genevieve*, whose snout-like cutterhead bores into the riverbed sand, and the propeller-driven *Ockerson*, called a "dustpan" because her huge scoop sucks up silt like a vacuum cleaner.

On the other hand the Corps's snagboat *Arkansas II* is fully recognized in river steamboat archives. Given dramatic mobility by her great sternwheel, she patrols her section of the Mississippi to clear snags and set out buoys—at the risk of her life: even in these photographs her steel hull was worn dangerously thin by scouring from river sand.

OCKERSON: OFF MEMPHIS

FROM THE SPLASHBOARD: THE MISSISSIPPI

85

PASSENGER FERRIES

DUTCHESS

Aside from the big luxury steamers, no other form of public transportation has been more vulnerable to today's modes of travel than the passenger ferryboat, which, until the widespread construction of superbridges, causeways and traffic tunnels, was the most familiar of all vessels. Harbors, bays, sizable streams had their ferries. Indeed, what growing riverbank community did not feel the need to have a boat-landing on its waterfront—as witness the signs for Ferry Street in so many of our smaller towns?

At this writing steam passenger ferries ply only three North American rivers: the St. Lawrence, the Mississippi and the lower Hudson. San Francisco Bay has none, neither does Boston nor Philadelphia: of all the harbors once crisscrossed by these ubiquitous shuttles, only in New York City's can they be found today. They survive because of legal red tape involved in discontinuing service, or because an alternate route has so far been impossible, or because their traffic is not heavy enough to warrant replacing them with a bridge or a tunnel.

The double-ended ferry is a fine demonstration of steamboat diversification, and takes advantage of the reciprocating engine's uniqueness, for basically it travels in the forward position in one direction, and makes the return trip in reverse—but at the same speed; and the only changes required are to shift some levers in the engineroom and to switch from one pilothouse to another.

Single-enders do not travel on this push-me-pull-you principle, so must turn around on their crossings, and then sidle up broadside to dock instead of nosing into a slip. This means that automobiles have to be driven around the center section of the vessel, and, to disembark, often face a cranky maneuver onto the ramp by which they boarded.

Following are a typical river ferry (on the Hudson), examples from the New York Harbor area, and some highly specialized single-ended individuals on the St. Lawrence and Mississippi rivers.

AT BEACON, NEW YORK

HUDSON RIVER

The Newburgh-Beacon Ferry will always represent for me the essence of river ferryboating in America. Although it was the last "upriver" ferry operation across the Hudson, it could have been anywhere; and its three little steam-driven double-enders burning hand-fired coal, its crews, its ferryhouses, its setting—all were perfection.

When the line stopped running on November 3, 1963, it severed a simple human contact that had existed since the original service was chartered in 1743, for the bridge replacing the *Dutchess*, *Orange* and *Beacon* not only by-passes Newburgh and Beacon but allows no foot travelers. Bells tolled in mourning when the boats made their last-day crossings, and since then the towns have stared at each other as strangers from opposite banks of their river.

ORANGE

AT NEWBURGH

90

NEWBURGH-BEACON FERRY

91

ELMIRA

Although recently each year has brought an end to another of her ferry operations, New York City remains the undisputed ferryboat capital of North America. At this writing there are seven separate crossings in the Harbor area, with steam used regularly on two of the three lines serving the public.

Happily, the finest passenger ferries afloat are among these public carriers: the Erie-Lackawanna Railroad's sisters *Elmira*, *Binghamton*, *Pocono* and *Scranton*. Built sixty-odd years ago, these gracious boats—coal-fired, tall-stacked, their lovely woodwork unspoiled—shuttle commuters across the mouth of the Hudson between Hoboken and lower Manhattan five days a week, twelve hours a day.

Other outstanding examples, some of them now gone, are the Jersey Central Railroad's *Wilkes-Barre*, the New York Central's *Stony Point*, the city-owned *Knickerbocker* on the famed Staten Island Ferry, and the U.S. Army's *Gen. Wm. H. Hart* to Governors Island.

N.Y.C. HARBOR

EVENING RUSH HOUR FROM MANHATTAN

94

FROM HOBOKEN

ELMIRA

MIDDAY LULL

SCRANTON

STATEN ISLAND FERRY

FROM GOVERNORS ISLAND

NYCRR STONY POINT

AT JERSEY CITY

The world's most romantic harbor ferries crosshatched San Francisco Bay for a century, but now all that remains of them physically is a vast graveyard of rotting hulks under the shadow of Golden Gate Bridge. Who knows when all steam ferries will leave New York City's harbor, too, and end like this derelict on the Jersey shore?

SAUSALITO, CALIFORNIA

Almost, just almost, were lovers of steam able to save the sidewheel walking-beam ferry *Brinckerhoff* as the museum piece she certainly was. But despite their efforts she was destroyed by court order, and her only epitaph is the signs for Brinckerhoff Street in a New York riverbank town.

BRINCKERHOFF

ST. LAWRENCE RIVER

Striking examples of diversification are North America's only "goose-egg" ferryboats, which shuttle year round between Quebec and Lévis. The line operating this unique type of single-ender uses sharp-prowed and armored vessels when the river freezes, and puts on airy, beautifully sponsoned boats for the warm months.

AT NEW ORLEANS

EDWIN N. BISSO.

LEO B. BISSO

The four existing center-paddlewheelers—the catamaran type developed more than a hundred years ago for shallow Western streams—are, fittingly, to be found on the Mississippi. Working within eighty miles of each other, these single-enders represent the only two steam ferry lines remaining in the entire watershed.

At New Orleans the feathered stacks and ornate pilothouses of *Edwin N. Bisso* and *Leo B. Bisso* are reminders of the old river tradition. Upstream at the capital the *City of Baton Rouge* and the *Louisiana* still puff gently back and forth, producing twin bow waves with their catamaran hulls.

110

LOUISIANA

LOUISIANA

CITY OF BATON ROUGE

LOCOMOTIVES

While there are still a few steamboats left in regular service on North American waters, comparable steam has vanished from this continent's major rails. Some of the surviving steam locomotives are on a dwindling handful of off-the-beaten-path lines where, forgotten by most of us, they have become curiosities employed in a service too marginal to warrant investment in any kind of modernity. Also, largely through the efforts of the never-say-die buffs, a few have been saved from the scrap-heap to run again on fan trips or on a score of new lines organized especially for steam excursions. However these events are more akin to antique-car meets than they are a re-creation of the days of steam railroading when the locomotive was an authentic part of our landscape and of the daily lives of its people. That era is now irrevocably gone.

The steam locomotive had a more far-reaching effect on the development of the continent than did any other piece of machinery. Within fifty years after its introduction it had formed a land transportation system unparalleled in history. For one brief century and a quarter it was the undisputed ruler of North America.

Of all the machines by which man has harnessed the elements to produce power, none can compare, to my mind, with the steam locomotive. This successor to the beast of burden was itself a creature—a metal beast, breathing steam instead of air; a glorious beast, which hissed and sighed and roared its way across the countryside. It was alive and proud, the embodiment of sheer brute force even in repose. Its mechanism of motion—never hidden beneath a shroud as are so many of today's contrivances—was completely exposed. This openness made it uniquely comprehensible, and took away anything sinister about its nature.

And naturally even more so than the casual viewer could the men who ran it and tended it feel its majestic vitality. Into its own intimate world of the engine terminal the sweaty creature was brought by the crew under whose hands it had toiled, and now, at rest, benignly allowed itself to be groomed and fed. Here in a place of smoke and grime and noise the chosen few who maintained it performed the constant rituals observed everywhere throughout the era of steam railroading—the cleaning of the fires; the taking of water, of coal, of sand; the washing and trimming and oiling; the turning-round, the checking and the polishing.

The most profound difference between the steam locomotive and the steamboat is that the former was solely a power plant, and served a single function: moving trains of cars that were not part of the engine itself. As the preceding photographs show, the steamboat's functions were so highly diversified that each type was designed for a specific performance; any change in its service almost always required extensive alterations that greatly altered its appearance.

Thus while there is no single boat which can stand for all steamboats, there can, I think, be a "universal" locomotive. Whether large or small, all steam locomotives had *fundamentally* the same shape no matter what service they performed. Even an engine designed for hauling fast passenger trains—and differing from its freight or switching counterparts in such things as overall size, diameter and arrangement of its wheels, tender capacity, and other minor mechanical modifications—could, if the need arose, perform another engine's task even when not perfectly suited to the role. The universal nature of this magnificent beast is further attested by the fact that dual-service engines could be designed that were, for example, equally at ease with the crack Empire Builder or with a heavy grain drag.

It is also true that particular locomotives shared unmistakable family resemblances, had traits that were the hallmark of each railroad and modifications adapting them to the conditions they were to meet on the line. But I feel that these differences and minor variations are appreciated only by the connoisseur; to most of us the essence of the steam locomotive is always the same. And certainly from a photographic standpoint the generic aspects common to all locomotives enable an individual to give a valid impression of what the entire species was like. It is this universality which I have tried to capture in the following pages, and which allows me to dispense with explanatory text to accompany the pictures.

One comment is apropos here, however. By the spring of 1960 all the large railroads in the United States and Canada had been Diesel-ized. During the period just prior to that date there were only three major railways on the continent still regularly using steam: the Norfolk & Western, the Grand Trunk Western, and the Canadian Pacific. Because, of the three, the CPR operated the greatest variety of engines in the greatest variety of services, and because it was the road with whose operations I was the most familiar, I chose to concentrate my picture-taking in the Atlantic Region, its last steam stronghold. Therefore a number of photographs are concerned with the atmosphere leading up to the last mainline regular service steam run made in the United States—by CPR Train No. 518, on March 27, 1960.

114

CANADIAN NATIONAL SWITCHER

CENTRAL VERMONT RAILWAY: ROUNDHOUSE

ST LUC ROUNDHOUSE

118

IN THE GLEN, MONTREAL

CPR WORKHORSE

VIRGINIA BLUE RIDGE: HOSING DOWN

READING: NO. 2124, TRIMMING

DRAWING THE FIRE AT ST LUC

CPR: NO. 2467, OILING ROUND

AT MC ADAM, NEW BRUNSWICK

124

BLOWING DOWN THE BOILER

125

GREAT NORTHERN: WILLMAR, MINNESOTA

TAKING WATER ON THE QUEBEC CENTRAL

DENVER & RIO GRANDE WESTERN: SANDING

CROSSHEAD AND CYLINDER OF A CONSOLIDATION

WHITE RIVER JUNCTION, VERMONT

CANADIAN NATIONAL: NO. 6218

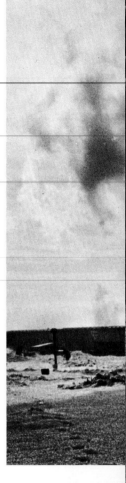

READING YARD, RUTHERFORD, PENNSYLVANIA

CPR READY TRACK

THE GLEN, MONTREAL

133

TEN BELOW AT VAUDREUIL

134

READING: THE SCHUYLKILL VALLEY

VIRGINIA BLUE RIDGE: ALONG THE JAMES RIVER

137

CPR: EXTRA 1217 EAST

GREAT NORTHERN: GRAIN EXTRA EAST

QUEBEC CENTRAL: EXTRA WEST

CPR: ENGINEER'S SIDE

THE FIREMAN'S SIDE

REPAIRS ON THE PETTICOAT PIPE

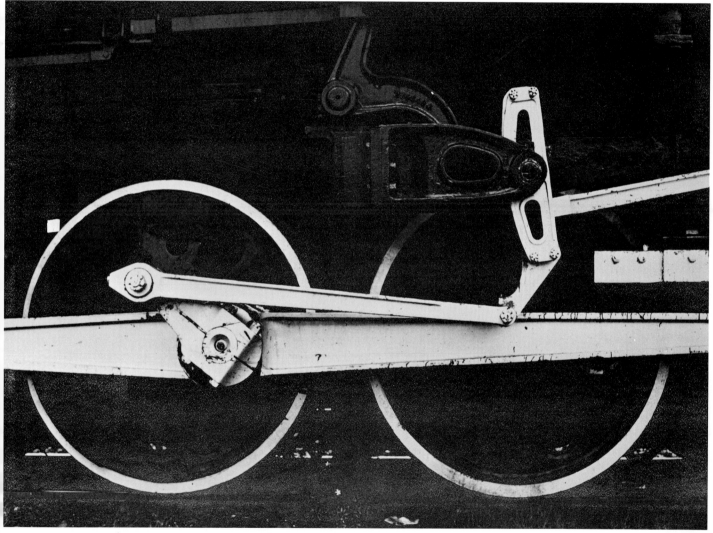

READING: A NORTHERN'S DRIVERS

143

AFTER THE RUN FROM HOCHELAGA

144

LOCUST GAP, PENNSYLVANIA

146

A scattering of railroad companies and lines organized to run excursion trains have given a few of steam engines a second lease on life. While a far cry from railroading in the classic sense, such operations have reprieved magnificent creatures like the Reading's 2100 and the Canadian National's 6218.

BRAINTREE, VERMONT

147

The *coup de grâce* can come swiftly for gallant engines if the price for scrap is high. Otherwise they linger in anguish on the "dead tracks," waiting to learn if they are to be spared as serviceable or as museum pieces, or must be consigned, stripped and crumbling, to a common grave.

AWAITING THE VERDICT

149

THE ANGUS SHOPS

151

NOTES

These comments follow the sequence according to the first appearance of the individual steamboats and locomotives, with subsequent photographs cited by page references.

Richelieu (Title-page; telegraph, Contents; pp. 13–19): Built 1913 by Harlan & Hollingsworth Corp. She, *Tadoussac* and *St. Lawrence* each carried *c.* 500 passengers, crew of *c.* 300, plus passengers' autos. As of 1966 all three unscheduled for any type of service, even freight. Photographs 8/64.

Keewatin (pp. 3, 5–8, 10, 12): With sister *Assiniboia* built 1907 by Fairfield Shipbuilding & Engineering, Glasgow. Always on service from Port McNicoll, Ont. (Georgian Bay, L. Huron) to Ft. William, "head of the Lakes." Operated April-Nov., carrying only cargo outside passenger season (June to mid-Sept.). North America's last boat train ran from Toronto to dockside Pt. McNicoll and return. Since main text written she has been scrapped because coal-burning. All photographs 9/64.

Assiniboia (pp. 4, 6, 9, 11): For builder, route, service see *Keewatin*, preceding. Stack shortened by one section when converted to oil. Not down at stern (viz. *Keewatin*) because end of run, fuel tank empty; cargo forward balances heavy engines aft. Will remain at least 1966 in freight service thanks to oil-burning. Photographs 9/64.

Tadoussac (pp. 20–23, 25): Built 1929; very different from *Richelieu* (q.v., Title-page, etc.). Photographs 8/64.

St. Lawrence (p. 24): Built 1929, but not identical sister of *Tadoussac*, preceding. Photograph 8/64.

Delta Queen (pp. 26–29): With identical *Delta King* prefabricated Scotland, assembled 1927 at Stockton for River Lines of San Francisco, provided overnight Sacramento R. service S.F.-Sacramento. Served U.S. government as barracks boats WW II, after which *King* abandoned. *Queen* bought 1947 by Greene Lines of Cincinnati, refurbished, placed on present extensive cruises (trips up to three weeks) on Mississippi, Ohio, Kentucky, Tennessee rivers. Photographs 9/64.

Belle of Louisville (pp. 30–33): Built 1914 originally as short-stacked ferry *Idlewild* by James Reese for W. Memphis Packet Co.; bought as *Avalon* by Jefferson Cy. for $34,-000; refitted (plus feathered stack sections added for atmosphere), began as *Belle* 1963. Averages two daily trips early spring-late fall, plus charters. Pilothouse amidships (traditional aft-of-stacks arrangement) makes her a unique steam relict. Photographs 1964.

Alexander Hamilton (pp. 34–39): Built 1924; inclined triple-expansion engines run her sidewheels. Present owner Circle Line, runs her Memorial to Labor Day (to July 1 to Bear Mt. only), plus off-season charters. Hudson River Day Line went out 1949, subsequent ownerships retained HRDL name, but not old service. Included in text sidewheeler tally. Photographs 1953, 1965.

Peter Stuyvesant (1926) last boat built for HRDL.

City of Keansburg (pp. 40, 41): Built 1924; owner Keansburg (N.J.) Steamboat Co.; summer round trips *c.* four hours; departs Battery Park (Manhattan); charters to Bear Mountain (Hudson R.), Rye Beach. Future very shaky. Photographs 1964, 1965 (Bear Mt. Bridge).

Catskill (p. 42): Built 1924, only example old freight-boat type extant; owner Bridgeport & Port Jefferson Steamboat Co., auto ferry spring-Oct., four daily round trips midseason. Photograph 1965.

Nobska (p. 43): Built 1926; owner Woods Hole, Martha's Vineyard & Nantucket Steamship Authority; summer season only, two daily round trips. Photograph 1965

Spartan (distance, p. 44; 47, at left): Built 1952. One of seven owned by Chesapeake & Ohio RR (including sister *Badger*, built 1953); among last reciprocating-steam vessels launched in North America. C&O RR-ferry routes from Ludington, Mich., to Wis.—Kewaunee, Manitowoc, Milwaukee (*Spartan* regularly to Milwaukee). Photographs 9/63.

Diamond Alkali (distance, p. 45; 47, at right): Built 1917 at Ecorse, Mich.; now owned by American Steamship Co. Example of self-unloading type of Laker (this feature probably added after construction). Photographs 9/63.

William J. Filbert (p. 46): Built 1907, Lorain, O.; owner U.S. Steel Corp. Like all Laker cargo-carriers, runs only in ice-free shipping season. Photograph 1964.

Algosoo (p. 48): Built 1901; present owner Algoma, Central & Hudson Bay RR, Sault Ste Marie, Ont. Counterstern a classic feature of large (propeller) steamboats this vintage (viz. *Keewatin*, *Assiniboia*). May be retired, as modernizing fleet. Photograph 9/64.

Ann Arbor No. 7: (pp. 49, 52): Built 1927, Manitowoc, Wis.; operates on any of RR's crossings (from Frankfort to Manistique or Menominee, Mich., or to Kewaunee or Manitowoc, Wis.). Since 1965 rebuilding and Diesel-izing, M/V *Viking*. Photographs 9/63.

Ann Arbor No. 5 (pp. 50, 51, 53): Built 1910 at Toledo Shipyards, hull No. 118; is only one of AA's four-boat fleet not extensively modernized since merger with Detroit, Toledo & Ironton RR in 1964. Photographs 9/63.

Chief Wawatam (pp. 54–57): Built 1911 Toledo Shipyards; hull no. (119) consecutive to *Ann Arbor No. 5*'s; only bow-loading RR-car ferry on Lakes. Owned by Mackinaw Transportation Co., St Ignace, Mich.; makes daily round trip ex-Sunday to Mackinaw City, providing only RR freight-car interchange between Michigan's upper and lower peninsulas. Photographs 9/63.

Lansdowne (pp. 58–61): Built 1884; engines 1872. Acquired with *Huron* by CNR at its formation 1923; carried RR passenger cars until 1955, now only freight cars; long converted to oil; great paddleboxes undecorated. Works winters on interchange between Grand Trunk Western (Detroit) and GTW owner CNR (Windsor); many trips daily, six days a week. Since photographs (4/64) two stacks have been removed.

Huron (pp. 62–63): Built 1875; non-condensing engines; very early propeller makes her far ahead of her time in design; now converted to oil. (For ownership and route see *Lansdowne*, preceding.) Summer spare boat. Photograph 9/63.

Manitowoc (p. 63): Built 1926, Manitowoc, Wis., for Wabash Rwy (since merged with Norfolk & Western). Ferries only RR freight cars Detroit-Windsor. Photograph 9/63.

New York Central RR Tugs: All built 1901–1924. *No. 31* (pp. 66–67); *No. 18* (pp. 68–69, top 71), off "North"—i.e. Hudson—piers; *No. 10* (lower, p. 71), built 1901; *No. 24* and *No. 32* (p. 72). All photographs 1963.

Bronx (p. 74): Built 1911; moved car floats on Harlem River Transfer (where swing bridges not obliged to open for her, viz. her short stack). Sold in merger of DL&W with Erie RR 1960. Resold down-country and Diesel-ized. Photograph 1959.

Victor (pp. 75–77): Built *c.* 1924 originally for Lehigh Valley RR. Petterson (New York City) also owns *Blairstown*, ex-Delaware, Lackawanna & Western; *Aqua*, ex-NYCRR waterboat, owned by Bay Ridge Water & Lighterage Co. Photographs 7/59, 1962.

Lone Star (pp. 78–81): Hull 1890, present superstructure 1922; owned by Miss E. Delarue (Builders Sand & Gravel Co. of Davenport); operates 20 miles north, 5 or 6 miles south of Davenport. Photographs 9/64.

The other two sternwheelers reportedly on similar service are the *Portland*, on Willamette R. at Portland, Ore., and a running-mate. Neither is comparable to *Lone Star*.

Ste. Genevieve (p. 82): Built 1932; owned U.S. Army Engineers, assigned to St. Louis Dist.; works the Mississippi (Cairo-St. Louis) and the Ohio (Cairo-Louisville). Omitted from paddlewheeler tally in main text. Photograph 10/64.

(Three Corps sidewheel dredgers are rumored working the Missouri R. area; but I've been unable to find them, and will welcome information on their existence.)

Ockerson (p. 83): Built 1932; assigned to Memphis Dist. Engineers; soon to be retired. Photograph 10/64.

Arkansas II (pp. 84, 85): Built 1940; last steam snagboat on Mississippi System; to date, last steam sternwheeler built in North America. Recognized by both *Inland River Record* and *Waterways Journal*, but not by Steamboat Historical Society; omitted from paddlewheel-

152

er tally. Assigned to Memphis Dist. Engineers to work Mississippi, White, Arkansas rivers. Supposedly removed from service 1965. Photograph 10/64.

Only other steam snagboat is Corps's sternwheeler *Montgomery*, built *c.* 1926, operating Florida-Georgia-Alabama.

Dutchess (p. 86): Built 1910, bought 1956 by N.Y. State Bridge Authority; superstructure rebuilt 1961. Scrapped after service discontinued. Photograph 11/63 arriving at Beacon.

Before bridge opened upstream *Dutchess*, *Orange* and spare summer boat *Beacon* (built 1921) carried yearly around 460,000 vehicles and 400,000 pedestrians.

Orange (pp. 88, 89): Built 1914, bought 1956 with *Dutchess* and *Beacon* from Newburgh-Beacon Ferry by N.Y. State Bridge Authority. After 11/63 sold for special trips out of Jersey City, where vandalized early 1966, sold for scrap. Photographs 1959–1963.

Elmira (p. 92; 97, distance): One of four built 1904–05 as commuter ferries for then Delaware, Lackawanna & Western RR (now Erie-Lackawanna). Operates with identical sisters *Binghamton, Pocono, Scranton* and two others on line's one remaining crossing from passenger-train terminal Hoboken, N.J., to Barclay St., Manhattan, 7 A.M. to 7 P.M. five days a week. All photographs 1960-61.

Binghamton (p. 93): see *Elmira*, preceding.

Pocono (pp. 96–97; 98, top); see *Elmira*.

Scranton (p. 98, lower): see *Elmira*, earlier.

Wilkes-Barre (p. 99): Built 1904; remodeled 1950's. Operated with four virtually identical boats, same vintage, by Central RR of New Jersey (Jersey Central) on Jersey City- Liberty St. (lower Manhattan) crossing. All but one retired spring 1965 when CNJ introduced leased Diesels. CNJ ferry line expected to discontinue by end of 1966 or shortly thereafter. Photograph 1/64.

Knickerbocker (p. 100, top): Built 1930, one of three identical twin-stackers Tompkinsville Class owned/run by N.Y. City Dept. of Marine & Aviation on Staten Island Ferry between St. George, Staten I., and South Ferry, Manhattan. She and sisters *Dongan Hills* and *Tompkinsville* (first-built of trio) probably U.S.A.'s most famous ferryboats; all replaced spring 1965 on receipt of crossing's first Diesels. Photograph 6/63.

Gen. Wm. H. Hart (p. 100, lower): Built 1925 for N.Y. City Dept. of Marine & Aviation as one of three in M&A's class of vest-pocket, twin-stacks-athwartships "institutional" ferryboats; now only active steam example. Bought by U.S. Government 1951; spare boat on nonpublic crossing from South Ferry, Manhattan, to Army's base on Governors Island. U.S. Coast Guard to take over ferry line's operation when base closes 6/66, may keep her on. Photograph 5/62.

Stony Point (p. 101): Built pre-WW I; with sisters *Weehawken, Utica* and *Niagara* remained on NYCRR's Weehawken ferry line (across lower Hudson) until service ended 3/59. Only *Niagara* in use: now (engineless) is

floating office for N.J. Public Service Co. See also *Albany*, following. Photograph 1958.

Albany (pp. 102–103): Last-built (1925) of quintet on NYCRR's Weehawken Ferry. Photograph 1962. Dead running-mate *Weehawken* lying near by; see *Stony Point* earlier.

San Francisco Bay Graveyard (p. 104): Photograph 7/62, when many boats serving as temporary pads for artists' colony. Last walking-beam engine to work in North America was on S.F. Bay in sidewheel ferry *Eureka* (not shown), retired *c.* 1956.

Brinckerhoff (p. 105): Built 1899; until 1946 (with brief hiatus) Hudson River ferry, Poughkeepsie-Highland (where street named for her); operated 1946-50 Long Island Sound between Bridgeport (Conn.)-Pleasure Beach. Acquired by Steamboat Historical Society, given to Mystic (Conn.) Seaport Marine Historical Assn. for preservation/exhibition in museum. Beached on Pawcatuck River bank and 3/65, over protests of steamboat fans, she and her beautiful engine were legally burned. Photograph 12/63.

Cité de Lévis (p. 106): Built 1930, Clydeside, by Napier & Miller; operated by La Traverse de Lévis Ltée. Identical sister and winter running-mate, *Cité de Québec*. Photograph 1964.

To my knowledge the only passenger ferry in North America having two (seasonal) sets of boats, and the only steam passenger-and-auto ferry operation on a Canadian river.

Bienville (p. 107): See *Cité de Lévis*, preceding. Scottish-built (Napier & Miller) 1925. Quite different summer running-mate, *Louis Joliet*, built 1938. Photograph 8/64.

Edwin N. Bisso and *Leo B. Bisso* (pp. 108, 109); Built *c.* 1926 for Bisso Ferry Co., New Orleans, for daily crossings at the foot of Jackson Ave. Marginal operation, future uncertain. Photographs 10/64.

City of Baton Rouge (pp. 110, 113): Built 1914 for Baton Rouge Transportation Co.; with younger *Louisiana* provides daily service Baton Rouge-Port Allen; both unspoiled by any modernization. Operation ceases with opening of new bridge, nearly completed. Photographs 10/64.

Louisiana (pp. 111, 112): Built 1924. See *City of Baton Rouge*, preceding. Photographs 10/64.

Duluth, Missabe & Iron Range RR *No. 220* (Title-page): Type 2-8-8-4 Yellowstone class M-3; built Baldwin Locomotive Wks 1941 as first of 18 for DM&IR; hauled up to 180 ore cars from Mesabe, etc., ranges to Duluth or Two Harbors, Mich. Yellowstones second-largest steam engines ever built (Union Pacific's 4-8-8-4 Big Boys largest). Photograph 5/56, Two Harbors.

Bonhomie & Hattiesburg Southern Rwy *No. 250* (Contents page): Rare 2-6-2 Prairie type; now on fan trips for Wannamaker, Kempton & Southern (Penna.). Photograph 10/63.

Canadian Pacific Rwy *No. 5145* (p. 115; drivers p. 144): A 2-8-2 P class Mikado on the Hochelaga Transfer leaves CPR St Luc

(freight) yard, Montreal; p. 144, St Luc enginehouse after return. Built mid-1930's CPR Angus Shops. Photographs 3/60.

Canadian National Rwys Switcher (p. 116): An 0-8-0 backing out of roundhouse, Hamilton, Ont.; photographed May 10, 1959, during last week of steam operation out of Hamilton (following week CN Diesel-ized all operations east of Fort William, Ont.).

Central Vermont Rwy *No. 470* (p. 117; crosshead p. 128): One of CV's 16 N-5a class 2-8-0 Consolidations, on local freight to Palmer, Mass.; a standard CV engine for light freight; built by American Locomotive Wks, Schenectady, N.Y., 1923. Photographs Brattleboro 2/57 during last week of steam operation.

St Luc Roundhouse/Yard (pp. 118 top, 119, 120 bottom, 121, 133 top, 142, 144, 145, 149): CPR's main freight yard and engine terminal in hub Montreal area. Here was the last large concentration of steam in eastern North America. Photographs 3/60.

The Glen (lower p. 118; 124; lower 133; 140): CPR's passenger-engine terminal at Westmount, Montreal area. Serviced all passenger engines; last were those on the local train around Montreal 3/60, when photographed.

CPR *No. 1262* (pp. 119; top 133, in center): A 4-6-2 Pacific type class G-5c, built 1946 by Montreal Locomotive Wks. G-5's (102 built 1944-48) designed to replace almost identical (even to high stacks!) engines *c.* 30-40 years old in light and branch-line freight/passenger service; several now on U.S. excursion lines. Photographs St Luc 3/60.

Virginia Blue Ridge Rwy *No. 8* (pp. 120 top; 137): Ex-U.S. Army standard 0-6-0, built 1942 American Locomotive Wks. VBR bought four in 1950's, used until 6/63. Primarily switcher, very light. Photographs 6/61.

Reading RR *No. 2124* (drivers p. 120, middle; foreground p. 132): Built 1947 at Rdg Shops, Reading (Penna.); one of thirty 4-8-4 Northern type class T-1's built 1945-47 (actually rebuilt older 2-8-0's). One of last steam engines constructed U.S.; used mainline freight until Rdg Diesel-ized. Four rebuilds (*Nos. 2100-2102, 2124*) saved, all but *No. 2101* used Iron Horse Rambles for next three years; *No. 2124* now at "Steamtown, U.S.A." (N. Walpole, N.H.); others await disposition in Reading. Photographs 9/63.

CPR *No. 2467* (p. 121, drivers): Built 1948, Montreal Locomotive Wks; one of 173 G-3 class 4-6-2 Pacific types built for CPR mid-1920's to 1948. Both freight and passenger service (CPR one of few RR's using 4-6-2's in freight); used Montreal to Rigaud and Vaudreuil (Canada's last steam passenger service) until Diesel take-over 1960. Photograph St Luc 3/60.

McAdam, N.B. (pp. 122–123): Hub of operations for CPR's Atlantic Region; major yard and engine terminal. Photograph 8/59.

CPR *No. 2412* (pp. 124–125, 140): Built 1942 Canadian Locomotive Wks, Kingston, Ont.; 4-6-2 Pacific class G-3g at St Luc. See CPR *No. 2467*, earlier. Photograph 3/60.

153

Great Northern Rwy *No. 3396* (p. 125): Built 1932, GN Superior (Wis.) Shops; one of 25 class O-8 2-8-2 Mikados (world's heaviest, most powerful 2-8-2's); oil-burning (like most GN steam engines). *No. 3396* in mainline freight service east of Minot, N.D.; last used Willmar (Minn.) Division. Photograph 2/56, while I was Asst. to Trainmaster of GN's Willmar Div. 1955–56.

Quebec Central Rwy *No. 1083* (p. 126): D-10k class 4-6-0 Tenwheeler, built 1912 at American Locomotive Wks for CPR's New England lines. Transferred after 1956 to QCR (part of CPR Atlantic Region, so also used many CP lettered engines, tenders). Photograph 3/60 Vallée Jct., P.Q., where she then a switcher.

Denver & Rio Grande Western RR *No. 494* (pp. 127, sanding; 135): Narrow-gauge K-37 class 2-8-2 built 1928 at D&RGW's Burnham Shops, Denver, as rebuild from standard-gauge 2-8-0 (all ten of RR's *490*'s so built, last four 1930). D&RGW last concentration active steam in North America (until recently 22 engines); operates 295-mile ng system on western Colo.-N.M. border, including passenger train Durango-Silverton (Colo.) during summer tourist season. On p. 135 *No. 494* on point (*No. 483* unseen, pushing), climbing 4% grade to top of Cumbres Pass, Colo. (10,015 ft.). Photographs 8/62.

Central Vermont Rwy *No. 707* (p. 129): Built 1928 by American Locomotive Wks; 2-10-4 Texas type class T-3; one of 10 built for heavy freight Brattleboro-St. Albans (largest steam engines in New England). All but *707* scrapped mid-1950's when CV Diesel-ized through freight service; she became legendary as spare engine when anything happened to Diesels, or

an extra called. Photograph 2/57 on her last trip into White River Junction. Scrapped several years later, after rusting in St. Albans.

Canadian National *No. 6218* (drivers pp. 130–131; p. 147): Built 1942 Montreal Locomotive Wks; 4-8-4 Northern type class U-2g. One of 203 CN 4-8-4's (world's largest fleet this type); mainline dual service—fastest passenger trains, heaviest freights. *No. 6218* only serviceable steam engine on CN roster, only currently operable mainline steam engine in Canada. Runs fan trips on Central Vermont (CNR subsidiary). Photographs 8/65.

Reading RR *No. 2100* (background p. 132; 136, 146): Photographed Rutherford, near Port Clinton, near Locust Gap (all Penna.), respectively, 9/63. For construction, use, etc., see *No. 2124*, earlier.

CPR *No. 2334* (top p. 133, at right): G-3d class 4-6-2 Pacific type, built 1926 Montreal Locomotive Wks. Photograph 3/60 St Luc yard just before retirement from freight service.

CPR *No. 2408* (lower p. 133, at left; 134): G-3g class 4-6-2 Pacific; built 1942 by Canadian Locomotive Wks, Kingston, Ont. (same order as *No. 2412*, p. 124). Photographs Vaudreuil, P.Q., 3/60. For service, etc., see *No. 2467*, earlier.

CPR *No. 2462* (lower p. 133, at right): One of several G-3 class Pacific type 4-6-2's on Canada's last steam passenger service. Photograph 3/60. See *No. 2467*, earlier,

Great Northern *No. 3377* (pp. 138–139, top): An O-8 class 2-8-2 built 1930 by GN Shops, Superior, Wis. For other data see *No. 3396*, earlier. Photograph 4/56 Kandiyohi, Minn.

CPR *No. 2541* (p. 139): Class G-2 4-6-2 Pacific type, built CPR Angus Shops 1908 (oldest locomotive in book). Photograph 3/60 near Tring Junction, P.Q., on her last local freight round trip on Quebec Central.

CPR *No. 1217* (pp. 138–139, bottom): A 4-6-2 Pacific G-5g, built 1945 Montreal Locomotive Wks. Photograph 3/60 arriving Vallée Jct., P.Q., from Thetford Mines to Quebec, on probably the last steam run of Quebec Central Rwy. See also *No. 1262*, earlier.

CPR *No. 5107* (both, p. 141): Photographs 3/27/60, Brownville Jct., Me., when she completed last steam locomotive run in mainline service in U.S. on CPR train No. 518 (scoot from Mégantic, P.Q.). At top, Moosehead Subdivision Engineer Bud Rolfe climbs down from cab of this Class P-1 2-8-2 Mikado built 1930 at CPR's Angus Shops.

CPR *No. 1263* (p. 142): See *No. 1262*, earlier.

Reading RR *No. 2102* (drivers p. 143): Photographed Macungie, Penna., 9/63. (Unseen p. 146 behind *No. 2100*). For construction use, etc., see *No. 2124*, earlier.

CPR *No. 2816* (p. 145): Built c. 1928; 4-6-4 Hudson type class H-1. Photograph 3/60 St Luc roundhouse after her last assignment.

CPR Angus Shops (pp. 148; 150–151): Montreal; CPR's main locomotive car shops; built engines until 1930's, thereafter a major point for scrapping locomotives—including many built there. Photograph 3/60.

CPR *No. 5449* (p. 149): Class P-2j 2-8-2 Mikado, built 1944 by Montreal Locomotive Wks; photographed 3/60 on the dead track, St Luc freight yard.

INDEX